BARACK OBAMA
IN HIS OWN WORDS

BARACK OBAMA
IN HIS OWN WORDS

Edited by
Lisa Rogak

CARROLL & GRAF PUBLISHERS
NEW YORK

Barack Obama in His Own Words

Published by
Carroll & Graf
An Imprint of Avalon Publishing Group, Inc.
245 West 17th Street, 11th Floor
New York, NY 10011

AVALON
publishing group incorporated

First Carroll & Graf edition 2007

ISBN-13: 978-0-78672-057-6
ISBN-10: 0-7867-2057-3

9 8 7 6 5 4 3 2 1

Interior design by *Ivelisse Robles Marrero*
Printed in the United States of America
Distributed by Publishers Group West

BARACK OBAMA
IN HIS OWN WORDS

Contents

The Quotes

Introduction

"WE ORIGINALLY SCHEDULED the Rolling Stones, but we canceled them when we figured out that Barack Obama would sell more tickets," New Hampshire governor John Lynch told Democratic supporters at the Senator's first appearance to test the waters in the state that's home to the first Presidential primary showdown.

Since delivering his keynote speech at the 2004 Democratic National Convention, Obama has been hailed as the clear savior of not only the Democratic party but of the integrity of American politics. Despite the fact that he burst onto the national scene seemingly overnight, his name recognition has grown by leaps and bounds ever since.

He hangs out with others with high name recognition, from the Reverend Rick Warren, author of *The Purpose Driven Life*, to Oprah and actors Matt Damon and George Clooney. Even investor Warren Buffett has gotten on board the Obama train.

Barack's lack of experience in the arena of national politics has not dissuaded Americans from believing that he would make a more than capable occupant of the nation's highest office, for a variety of reasons.

For one, he represents the American dream. He came from nothing, pulled himself up by his bootstraps after stumbling a few times, and now has a clear shot of winning the nation's highest office. Over several decades where the presidency has been characterized more often than not by scandal, overuse of power, and corruption, Obama is the total opposite, as sincere as they come, a rare bird inside the Beltway. Clearly, this is why his lack of national political experience appears to be a non-issue with many Americans. After all, the last few guys who have held the office had decades of experience and look where it got us. We might as well give the other side of the pendulum a try, goes the reasoning. At this point, it can't hurt, right?

The response to his books seems to bear this out. Obama's new book, *The Audacity of Hope: Thoughts on Reclaiming the American Dream*, hit number two on the *New York Times* bestseller list the first week it was published. Its success has naturally increased sales of his first book *Dreams From My Father*, published in 1995, which sold only a handful of copies when it first came out. In December 2004, Obama made a $1.9 million, three-book deal with Random House. *Audacity* was the first to be published, the second will be a children's book in 2007 co-written with his wife and two daughters, and the topic of the third title has not yet been announced. Undoubtedly when these books are published, they will also hit the bestseller lists and further boost his reputation and visibility.

Hype aside, most people don't know where Obama stands on the issues. *Barack Obama in His Own Words* will tell you. You can use this book to learn where the senator stands on the issues that matter most to Americans today, and to help decide if Barack Obama is the right candidate for you.

Barack Obama in Brief

BARACK OBAMA WAS born in Hawaii on August 4, 1961, to Barack Obama, Sr., an economics student and devout Muslim from Kenya, and Ann Dunham, a white woman from Kansas. His parents separated when Barack was two years old and ultimately divorced. After the divorce his father attended Harvard University to pursue a doctorate before eventually returning to Kenya. His mother remarried and moved to Indonesia when Barack was six. The family lived in Jakarta for four years, and Barack returned to Hawaii by himself to live with his grandparents until he graduated from high school in 1979. He attended Occidental College in California for two years before he transferred to Columbia University.

In 1982, he received word that his father had died in a car accident in Kenya, and it threw him for a loop despite the fact that he had only seen his father once since his parents' divorce, when Barack was ten. He graduated from Columbia with a bachelor's in political science in 1983. After spending a year in a corporate job, he moved to Chicago where he chose to work in community projects, joining a nonprofit organization involved in job training. In 1988, he enrolled at Harvard Law School, where he would first gain national recognition for serving as the first African-American president of the *Harvard Law Review*. After graduating *magna cum laude* from Harvard in 1991, Obama returned to Chicago to continue his work with community nonprofits as a civil rights lawyer and taught at the University of Chicago law school with a specialty in constitutional law. He met Michelle Robinson, another lawyer, in the summer of 1989 while they were working at a corporate law firm, and they married in 1992.

As a result of his visibility at Harvard, Random House asked him to write an autobiography, and *Dreams from My Father* was published in 1995. His mother, who had been diagnosed with cancer a few months earlier, died shortly after the book was published. He and Michelle have two daughters: Malia, born in 1999, and Sasha, born in 2001.

His first run at public office resulted in success when Barack won the election to represent the South Side of Chicago in the Illinois State Senate in 1996. He served until 2004, when he was elected to the U.S. Senate with 70 percent of the vote, becoming the fifth African-American in U.S. history to serve in the august chamber.

In the wake of his increasing national popularity, Barack recorded the audio version of his autobiography, *Dreams from My Father*, which won a Grammy Award for Best Spoken Word Album in 2006. He formed an exploratory committee to decide whether to run for president in 2008, and announced that he would formalize his plans in February 2007.

The Quotes

ON ABORTION

I think the Democrats historically have made a mistake just trying to avoid the issue or pretend that there's not a moral component to it. There is. I am pro-choice, but I also think that it's important—even as I indicate that I'm pro-choice—to say this is not a trivial issue. And we have to listen to the profound concerns that other people have.

Face the Nation, March 12, 2006

No one is pro-abortion.

Speech at Benedictine University, October 5, 2004

ON ABRAHAM LINCOLN

Lincoln was not a perfect man, nor a perfect president. By modern standards, his condemnation of slavery might be considered tentative.

Chicago Tribune, June 26, 2005

I'm fascinated by Lyndon Johnson; there's a piece of him in me. That kind of hunger—desperate to win, please, succeed, dominate—I don't know any politician who doesn't have some of that reptilian side to him. But that's not the dominant part of me. On the other hand, I don't know that it was the dominant part of Lincoln. The guy was pretty reflective.

Men's Vogue, Fall 2006

I cannot swallow whole the view of Lincoln as the Great Emancipator.

Time Magazine, June 26, 2005

ON AFGHANISTAN

I have always thought that we did the right thing in Afghanistan. My only concern with respect to Afghanistan was that we diverted our attention from Afghanistan in terms of moving into Iraq, and I think would could have done a better job of stabilizing that country than we have in providing assistance to the Afghani people. All of us should be rooting for the Afghani people and making sure that we are providing them the support to make things happen.

Illinois Senate Debate, Illinois Radio Network, October 12, 2004

ON AFRICA

Africans are going to have to be responsible for their own salvation. We have to be partners with them in that process. The African-American community here has to be attentive to their issues. On the flip side, African leaders have to create a rule of law that is not corrupt, that is transparent.

Essence, October 2006

Black Americans have always had an ambiguous relationship with Africa. Nowadays, we wear *kente* cloth, celebrate Kwanza and put up posters of Nelson Mandela on our walls. And when we travel to Africa and discover it's not all sweetness and light, we can end up deeply disappointed.

Crisis, October 1995

ON THE AFRICAN-AMERICAN COMMUNITY

I don't think the Democratic Party takes the African-American voters for granted. I want Republicans to compete for the African-American vote. They're not getting the African-American vote not because African-Americans aren't open-minded, but because Democrats have consistently championed those issues—civil rights, voting rights, concern for working families—that are of greatest concern to African-American voters.

Meet the Press, July 25, 2004

In the African-American community in particular, I think sometimes we have a tendency for our leadership to be very protective of their turf and not invite young people in until it's way too late. The earlier we're grooming young people and giving them leadership opportunities, and pushing them up front, the better.

Black Collegian, October 2006

I firmly believe the overwhelming majority of African-Americans are just as hardworking, just as intent to go about their business. What is true, though, is sometimes we get into the mode of it's easier to blame white folks for things than us taking the responsibility.

Who's Afraid of a Large Black Man? Charles Barkley, page 35

We have a certain script in our politics, and one of the scripts for black politicians is that for them to be authentically black they have to somehow offend white people. And then if he puts a multiracial coalition together, he must somehow be compromising the efforts of the African-American community. To use a street term, we flipped the script.

Chicago Tribune, June 26, 2005

I think that it is the best of times and the worst of times for the African-American community. And one of the things that I want to make certain is that the voices of young men standing on a street corner without hope and vision for the future. Voices are heard in the U.S. Senate, that we feel a certain sense of urgency about a generation that we're losing.

All Things Considered, July 27, 2004

Any black person in America who's successful has to be able to speak several different forms of the same language. You take on different personas as you need to, when you have to. There's nothing wrong with it. You're going to speak differently on the golf course with your golf buddies than you are with your buddies around the kitchen table.

Who's Afraid of a Large Black Man? Charles Barkley, page 25

I know if I'm in an all-black audience that there's going to be a certain rhythm coming back at me from the audience. They're not just going to be sitting there. That creates a different rhythm in your speaking.

Chicago Tribune, June 26, 2005

ON AIDS

We are all sick because of AIDS—and we are all tested by this crisis. Neither philanthropist nor scientist; neither government nor church, can solve this problem on their own—AIDS must be an all-hands-on-deck effort.

World AIDS Day Speech, December 1, 2006

I don't think we can deny that there is a moral and spiritual component to prevention. Again and again I heard stories of men and women contracting HIV because sex was no longer part of a sacred covenant, but a mechanical physical act. Having said that, I also believe that we cannot ignore that abstinence and fidelity may too often be the ideal and not the reality. If condoms and potentially microbicides can prevent millions of deaths, they should be made more widely available.

Orange County Register, December 1, 2006

ON THE AMERICAN DREAM

Stay amazed, and remain in wonder at this unlikely place we call America. I think it's easy for some people to look at all the challenges we face; to look at poverty and war and racism and inequality and hatred and helplessness, and to get down on this country as a result. To think that there's something wrong with us and that there is little hope to make things better. If you ever feel like that yourselves, I ask you to remember all the amazing and unlikely things that have happened in this country. This is America. A place where millions of restless adventurers from all over the world, still weary of their lot in life—still hoping for something better—have longed to travel great distances and take great risks for a chance to arrive on our shores.

University of Massachusetts at Boston Commencement Address,
June 2, 2006

This country remains the greatest on Earth, not because of the size of our military or the size of our economy, but because every child can actually achieve as much as they can dream.

Meet the Press, July 25, 2004

ON BEING A CHRISTIAN

You need to come to church in the first place precisely because you are first of this world, not apart from it. You need to embrace Christ precisely because you have sins to wash away—because you are human and need an ally in this difficult journey.

Call to Renewal Keynote Address, June 28, 2006

There are still passages that I read in the Bible where I say, Well, this doesn't make any sense.

New Yorker, October 30, 2006

We should never forget that God granted us the power to reason so that we would do His work here on Earth.

World AIDS Day Speech, December 1, 2006

My faith is one that admits some doubt.

ABC's *This Week with George Stephanopoulos*, August 15, 2004

ON BIPARTISANSHIP

Senator Tom Coburn of Oklahoma is the best kind of conservative because he's a sincere conservative. He's not just trying to score political points. We all have an interest in making sure our money is well spent.

Knight Ridder Tribune, October 20, 2006

I'm not somebody comfortable with liberal-conservative labels. What the American people are looking for are commonsense solutions.

Meet the Press, July 25, 2004

To me, the issue is not are you centrist or are you liberal? The issue to me is, Is what you're proposing going to work? Can you build a working coalition to make the lives of people better? And if it can work, you should support it whether it's centrist, conservative, or liberal.

New York Magazine, October 2, 2006

ON BLUE STATES AND RED STATES

With the red-state phenomenon where Democrats just say, well, we can't campaign in those areas because they're going to vote Republican, I think that's a mistake.

Face the Nation, March 12, 2006

There is a faction on the right that is very absolutist and there's a portion of the left that is the same way, demonizing the other side. And then there are eighty percent of people in the middle.

Rolling Stone, December 30, 2004

These either/or formulations are wearisome. They're not useful. The reality outstrips the mental categories we're operating in.

New York Magazine, October 2, 2006

ON BOOKS THAT HAVE INSPIRED HIM

I remember reading [Studs Terkel's] *Working* when it first came out and just finding that very powerful. What stuck was to reveal the sacredness of ordinary people's lives. That everybody has a story. And I think Studs is terrific at drawing out that shimmering quality of people's everyday struggles.

Chicago Tribune, October 26, 2006

Right around my first year of college, I read *Song of Solomon*, by Toni Morrison, it just moved me tremendously. The power of language and how it can peel back truths, bring things to the surface.

Chicago Tribune, October 26, 2006

ON CAMPAIGN FINANCE REFORM

Real reform means making sure that members of Congress and the administration tell us when they're negotiating for jobs with industries they're responsible for regulating. That way we don't have people writing a drug bill during the day and meeting with pharmaceutical companies about their future salary at night.

Speech to the Chicago Council on Foreign Relations, November 22, 2005

The underlying issue of how extensively money influences politics is the original sin of everyone who's ever run for office—myself included. In order to get elected, we need to raise vast sums of money by meeting and dealing with people who are disproportionately wealthy.

Speech at the Lobbying Reform Summit, January 26, 2006

The biggest advantage that big money has in Washington is a host of full-time lobbyists who can track that one bill that, for their client, means a billion-dollar tax break, but that nobody else even knows is there.

New Yorker, October 30, 2006

The whole issue of money in politics is one that I'm constantly struggling with, because my preference would be that we've got public financing of campaigns and nobody has to raise money whatsoever.

All Things Considered, October 19, 2006

Even if we pass a good bill and rid Washington of the Jack Abramoffs of the world, it's going to take much more than gift bans and lobbying reform to restore the public's faith in a government. It will take not simply a change in laws, but a change in attitudes. To earn back that trust—to show people that we're working for them and looking out for their interests—we have to start acting like it.

Speech to the Chicago Council on Foreign Relations, November 22, 2005

ON HIS CHILDHOOD

I was such a terror that my teachers didn't know what to do with me.

Harper's, November 2006

Growing up, I absorbed a lot of negative stereotypes about how I should behave as a black teenager and fell into some of the same traps that a lot of black male youth do. It wasn't preordained that I would go to Columbia or to Harvard. I didn't have a father in the house, which meant that I didn't have a lot of role models in terms of how I should operate.

Chicago Tribune, June 26, 2005

When I was a kid I inhaled. That was the point.

Economist, October 28, 2006

My mother taught me not to reject a compliment when it's offered.

Letter to *The Black Commentator*, June 19, 2003

ON HIS CHILDREN

My little girls can break my heart. They can make me cry just looking at them eating their string beans.

Houston Chronicle, October 29, 2006

One of the wrestling matches I'm always having with my staff is getting my kids' events onto the schedule. I have to make sure they understand that's a priority.

Live Your Best Life, Oprah Winfrey, page 294

When I sit down with my six-year-old and my three-year-old at night and I'm reading a book to them and then I tuck them in to go to sleep, that's a little piece of heaven that I hang onto.

American Libraries, August 2005

ON CHINA

The U.S. should be firm on issues that divide us [from the Beijing government]—like Taiwan—while flexible on issues that could unite us. We should insist on labor standards and human rights, the opening of Chinese markets fully to American goods, and the fulfillment of legal contracts with American businesses, but without triggering a trade war, as prolonged instability in the Chinese economy could have global economic consequences.

"Renewal of American Leadership" press release, July 12, 2004

ON HIS CIGARETTE HABIT

I smoked for a long time and quit, and occasionally I lapse back into it. It's an ongoing struggle.

Knight Ridder Tribune, October 20, 2006

I'm a reformed smoker; I think that surprises people. I quit, but then during the campaign when you're in a car driving through cornfields, occasionally I bum a cigarette or two. But I did all my drinking in high school and college. I was a wild man. I did drugs and drank and partied. But I got all my ya-yas out.

Rolling Stone, December 30, 2004

ON CONGRESS

This has been a very unproductive Congress since I've arrived there. Hopefully, though, there's no correlation between my arrival and the lack of productivity. I've been in the minority and I haven't been able to move a lot of legislation forward because frankly those who have been in charge of the Senate, the Republican majority, haven't been interested in the work that I've been doing.

Larry King Live, October 19, 2006

ON HIS CRITICS

It's not that I'm being cautious. It's that I disagree with them.

Time, February 20, 2006

ON THE CURRENT STATE OF POLITICS

It's 24-hour, slash-and-burn, negative-ad, bickering, small-minded politics that doesn't move us forward.

Milwaukee Journal Sentinel, December 11, 2006

Politics in Washington has become the intellectual equivalent of WWF Wrestling: smacking each other, throwing chairs, but nothing really gets done.

Houston Chronicle, October 29, 2006

ON DARFUR

We should be engaged in Darfur. We have a self-interest and a stake in preventing hundreds of thousands of people from being slaughtered.

New Yorker, January 15, 2007

The United States should raise the needed funds to ensure that the civilians in Sudan receive life-saving humanitarian assistance. We should lead in contributing the lion's share of these funds so that we can convince others to give their fair share as well. Next, the United States should support the immediate deployment of an effective international force to disarm militias, protect civilians, and facilitate delivery of humanitarian assistance in Darfur.

Speech, October 7, 2004

We have a strong national security interest. If you start seeing more and more failed states, more and more displaced persons, more and more refugees, all of that becomes a breeding ground for terrorist activity, it becomes a breeding ground for disease, and it creates refugees that put pressure on our own borders. In an interconnected world we can't insulate ourselves from these tragedies. We're going to have to develop some strategy as the world's remaining super-power to address these issues, and Darfur is an important test case. We've already failed one test in Rwanda, we shouldn't fail another.

"Darfur: Current Policy Not Enough" podcast, February 15, 2006

ON HIS DECISION TO RUN FOR PRESIDENT

This is a profoundly personal decision that I'm going through. I'm looking at the external factors: money, organization, calendar, all those things. But the most important thing I'm looking at is, Do I have something unique to bring to a presidential race that would justify putting my family through what I think everybody understands is a grueling process?

Chicago Tribune, November 20, 2006

I think I was first asked [if I was going to run for president] the day after I'd been elected to the Senate. It was an eight-in-the-morning press conference, I'd just come out of the election, and I remember laughing at the question because presumably it would make sense for me to be sworn into my new office before I started thinking about the next one.

All Things Considered, October 19, 2006

The decision to run for president is a very serious one. And it's a very humbling decision. I have to feel that I have something unique to offer the country that no other person can provide right now.

Ebony, February 2007

The one thing I'm clear about in terms of the presidency is that it can't be something you pursue on the basis of vanity and ambition. There's a certain soberness and seriousness required.

Meet the Press, October 22, 2006

What's happened is that we create this parlor game where, you know, there's constant speculation and is this person running, is this person not running. And then candidates who do decide to run end up stretching out their announcement over the course of the year and make four different announcements

All Things Considered, October 19, 2006

My general attitude is that if I'm doing a good job in what I'm doing now, I can have the opportunity to seek higher office. If I'm not doing a good job and paying too much attention to what could happen down the road, that option won't be open to me.

Essence, October 2006

Running for the presidency is a profound decision—a decision no one should make on the basis of media hype or personal ambition alone—and so before I committed myself and my family to this race, I wanted to be sure that this was right for us, and more importantly, right for the country.

Barackobama.com, January 16, 2007

I certainly didn't expect to find myself in this position a year ago. But as I've spoken to many of you in my travels, I've been struck by how hungry we all are for a different kind of politics.

USA Today, January 17, 2007

ON DEMOCRACY

There's always going to be some conflict in democracy. It's a big country. It's a complicated country. Democracy is messy. And a lot of that is healthy.

Charlie Rose Show, October 19, 2006

ON THE DEMOCRATIC PARTY

The belief in each other—that's what made me a Democrat.

San Francisco Chronicle, October 28, 2006

The party has not updated its vision and its message. We haven't painted a picture of where we want to take the country.

Essence, October 2006

This is our time and I'm grateful to be a part of that.

Democratic fundraiser in Manchester, New Hampshire,
December 12, 2006

The Democratic Party has always stood for giving everyone an equal chance, despite the circumstances of their birth. My story is emblematic of that. I want to affirm those values.

National Review, July 27, 2004

The Democratic Party has not told a good story. What we have are a series of policy prescriptions to solve particular issues. We have our environmental position and our labor position and our health-care position, but we don't have a narrative. And the Republicans do.

Rolling Stone, December 30, 2004

I think there's a false choice being presented in the Democratic Party right now, between those who argue that our job is to oppose everything George Bush does and cling to the old-time religion, or the faction where you just split the difference and not notice that over a number of years the goalposts are drifting further and further to the right. What I think we have to do is transcend those categories.

Time, February 13, 2006

There are times I think we're not ambitious enough. Back in 2004, one of the candidates had made a proposal about universal health care, and a commentator said, "We can't propose this kind of big-government costly program, because it'll send a signal we're tax-and-spend liberals." But that's not a good reason to not do something. You don't give up on the goal of universal health care because you don't want to be tagged as a liberal.

New York Magazine, October 2, 2006

If the Democrats can't inspire, if they can't tap into some sense of meaning that goes beyond just dollars and cents, then it's going to be very hard for them to argue against the sort of selfishness and self-interested policies that have come to dominate our politics.

All Things Considered, March 10, 2005

If the Democrats are only issuing white papers and policy positions and not talking to people about their central experiences, then I think there are going to be problems.

ABC This Week, November 7, 2004

We've got a story to tell that isn't just against something but is for something. We know that we're the party of opportunity.

Annual Take Back America Conference, June 14, 2006

We as Democrats have not been very interested in poverty or issues relating to the inner city as much as we should have. Think about the last presidential campaign: It's pretty hard to focus a moment on which there was any attention given.

Chicago Tribune, September 11, 2005

ON DIVERSITY

I believe in vigorous enforcement of our nondiscrimination laws. But I also believe that a transformation of conscience and a genuine commitment to diversity on the part of the nation's CEOs could bring about quicker results than a battalion of lawyers. They have more lawyers than us anyway.

Call to Renewal Keynote Address, June 28, 2006

Religious people are far more tolerant than I think the popular culture gives them credit for. Conversely, secularists are far more interested in morality and ethics than the right wing would portray them.

Charlie Rose Show, October 19, 2006

I'm well situated to help the country understand how we can both celebrate our diversity in all its complexity and still affirm our common bonds. Maybe I can help with that because I've got so many different pieces in me.

Life Your Best Life, Oprah Winfrey, page 293

ON EDUCATION

I think that community colleges are going to play an increasingly critical role, because one thing we know for certain about the changing economy is that nobody is going to have a permanent job.

Community College Week, March 28, 2005

No longer can we assume that a high-school education in Boston is enough to compete for a job that could easily go to a college-educated student in Bangalore or Beijing.

University of Massachusetts at Boston Commencement Address,
June 2, 2006

We have an obligation and a responsibility to be investing in our students and our schools. We must make sure that people who have the grades, the desire and the will, but not the money, can still get the best education possible.

Black Issues in Higher Education, October 7, 2004

It's really important that we revamp our college loan programs to free up more money for students. The direct loan program works extremely well, and there doesn't appear to be a need for these student loan programs to be managed through banks and other private lenders. If we were able to consolidate programs under the Direct Loan program, we would save $4.5 billion, which could be funneled back into providing more Pell grants and providing a higher level of grants per student.

Black Issues in Higher Education, October 7, 2004

No Child Left Behind did not speak to what I think is a critical issue in education, that is how do we encourage our best and brightest to continue teaching, and how do we substantially upgrade the pay and performance of the teaching profession?

Speech at the Aspen Institute, July 2, 2005

We know that in a global economy that's more connective and more competitive that we're the party that will guarantee every American an affordable, world-class, life-long, top-notch education, from early childhood to high school—from college to on-the-job training. We know that that's what we're about.

Annual 2006 Take Back America Conference, June 14, 2006

I try to avoid an either/or approach to solving the problems of this country. There are questions of individual responsibility and questions of societal responsibility to be dealt with. The best example is an education. I'm going to insist that we've got decent funding, enough teachers, and computers in the classroom, but unless you turn off the television set and get over a certain anti-intellectualism that I think pervades some low-income communities, our children are not going to achieve.

Meet the Press, July 25, 2004

Our public education system is the key to opportunity for millions of children and families. It needs to be the best in the world. Of particular concern is the growing achievement gap between middle- and low-income students, which has continued to expand despite some overall national achievement gains.

ObamaForIllinois.com, May 2, 2004

ON ENERGY POLICY

Here's the deal we can make with the auto companies. It's a piece of legislation I introduced called Health Care for Hybrids, and it would allow the federal government to pick up part of the tab for the auto companies' retiree health care costs. In exchange, the auto companies would then use some of that savings to build and invest in more fuel-efficient cars.

Speech at the Governor's Ethanol Coalition, February 28, 2006

Our persistent dependence on oil is a danger our government has known about for years. And despite constant warnings by researchers and scientists, major corporations and our own government officials, it's a danger they have failed to prepare for, listen to, or seriously try to guard against. It's a danger we can no longer afford to ignore.

"Securing Our Energy Future" speech, September 15, 2005

Saying that America is addicted to oil without following a real plan for energy independence is like admitting alcoholism and then skipping the 12-step program.

Chicago Tribune, April 3, 2006

[We should] free America from its dependence on foreign oil. We must take concrete steps to move us toward energy independence including requiring that 20 percent of the nation's power supply portfolio come from renewable sources like wind, solar, biomass, and geothermal energy by 2020, and that a percentage of our nation's fuel supply is provided by renewable fuels such as ethanol and biodiesel.

"Renewal of American Leadership" press release, July 12, 2004

I voted for the last energy bill because it took some baby steps in the right direction. It invests in the renewable, homegrown biofuels that could turn out to be some of the most promising alternatives to oil. The solutions are too timid, the reforms too small. A bill that reduces our dependency on foreign oil by just 3 percent when our demand is about to jump 40 percent is not a serious energy policy. We need to do more.

"Securing Our Energy Future" speech, September 15, 2005

We can't continue to settle for piecemeal, bite-sized solutions to our energy crisis. We need a national commitment to energy security, and to emphasize that commitment, we should install a Director of Energy Security to oversee all of our efforts. Like the Chairman of the Joint Chiefs and the National Intelligence Director, this person would be an advisor to the National Security Council and have the full authority to coordinate America's energy policy across all levels of government.

Speech at the Governor's Ethanol Coalition, February 28, 2006

We could save as much, in terms of our fuel, if we increased our fuel efficiency standards, as much as we would from getting Alaska drilling going immediately. And that's been the Bush strategy: increasing production for oil and gas companies, subsidizing them to the tune of 20 billion dollars, as opposed to thinking about how not only we can develop alternative fuels, but also how can we conserve energy and increase efficiencies available right now but have not been invested in.

Illinois Senate Debate, October 26, 2004

Let's fight to wean ourselves off Middle East oil, through an energy policy that doesn't simply serve the interests of Exxon and Mobil.

Speech at anti-Iraq War rally in Chicago, October 26, 2002

The only thing as predictable as rising gas prices are the short-term political solutions that usually come along with them. Every year you had the same headlines, Pain at the Pump, and then Americans start emptying their wallets to fill up their tanks and politicians go through the standard responses: tax rebates and tax holidays, investigating price-gouging bio-oil companies.

"A Real Solution for High Gas Prices" podcast, May 11, 2006

ON EQUAL RIGHTS

We must be careful to keep our eyes on the prize—equal rights for every American. We must continue to fight for the Employment Non-Discrimination Act. We must vigorously expand hate-crime legislation and be vigilant about how these laws are enforced. We must continue to expand adoption rights to make them consistent and seamless throughout all 50 states, and we must repeal the "Don't Ask, Don't Tell" military policy.

Windy City Times, February 11, 2004

ON FOREIGN POLICY

American leadership has been a mighty force for human progress. The steady march of democracy and free enterprise across the globe speaks to the steadfastness of our leadership and the power of our ideals. Today we face new and frightful challenges, especially the threat of terror. Never has it been more important for America to lead wisely, to shrewdly project power and wield influence on behalf of liberty and security. Unfortunately, I fear our once great influence is waning, a victim of misguided policies and impetuous actions. Never has the U.S. possessed so much power, and never has the U.S. had so little influence to lead.

Speech to the Chicago Council on Foreign Relations, July 12, 2004

It is absolutely vital that we maintain a strong and active foreign policy, relentless in pursuing our enemies and hopeful in promoting our values around the world.

St. Louis Post-Dispatch, November 20, 2006

I'm proud of the fact that I stood up early and unequivocally in opposition to Bush's foreign policy. That opposition hasn't changed.

Letter to *The Black Commentator*, June 19, 2003

The world is watching what we do today in America. They will know what we do here today, and they will treat all of us accordingly in the future—our soldiers, our diplomats, our journalists, anybody who travels beyond these borders. I hope we remember this as we go forward.

Floor Statement on the Habeas Corpus Amendment,
September 27, 2006

In every region of the globe, our foreign policy should promote traditional American ideals: democracy and human rights; free and fair trade and cultural exchanges; and development of institutions that ensure broad middle classes within market economies. It is our commonality of interests in the world that can ultimately restore our influence and win back the hearts and minds necessary to defeat terrorism and project American values around the globe. Human aspirations are universal—for dignity, for freedom, for the opportunity to improve the lives of our families.

Speech to the Chicago Council on Foreign Relations, July 12, 2004

I think [Americans] instinctively understand that we cannot simply impose our will militarily on the entire globe.

Houston Chronicle, October 29, 2006

People say, surely we can create a foreign policy and a national-security strategy that combines the might of our military with diplomacy. We've done it before. Why can't we do it again?

Seattle Times, October 27, 2006

We still have the chance to correct recent missteps that have put our principles and legacy in question. Indeed, it is imperative to our nation's standing and security to do so. It will take a change of attitude and direction in our national leadership to restore the values and judgment that made and kept our nation the world's beacon of hope and freedom.

Speech to the Chicago Council on Foreign Relations, July 12, 2004

ON FREE TRADE

[My constituents] wear Nike shoes and buy Pioneer stereos. They don't want the borders closed. They just don't want their communities destroyed.

New Yorker, May 31, 2004

ON THE FUTURE

It's not that ordinary people have forgotten how to dream. It's just that their leaders have forgotten how.

Philadelphia Inquirer, December 11, 2006

It's your turn to keep this daringly radical but unfailingly simple notion of America alive—that no matter where you're born or how much your parents have; no matter what you look like or what you believe in, you can still rise to become whatever you want; still go on to achieve great things; still pursue the happiness you hope for.

University of Massachusetts at Boston Commencement Address,
June 2, 2006

At their core Americans are a decent people. And there is a sense of hope that people can change this country together.

Times of London, December 11, 2006

The true test of the American ideal is whether we're able to recognize our failings and then rise together to meet the challenges of our time. Whether we allow ourselves to be shaped by events and history, or whether we act to shape them.

Knox College Commencement Address, June 4, 2005

ON GAY MARRIAGE

The heightened focus on marriage is a distraction from other, attainable measures to prevent discrimination of gays and lesbians.

The Audacity of Hope, pages 222-3

I am somebody who has not embraced gay marriage. I've said that it's not something that I think the society is necessarily ready for. And it strikes me that in a lot of ways for a lot of people, it may intrude in how they understand marriage. But I also think that we should create civil unions for gays and lesbians that allow them to have the same basic rights as all people.

Larry King Live, October 19, 2006

I don't think marriage is a civil right, but I think that not being discriminated against is a civil right.

Illinois Senate Debate, October 26, 2004

I opposed the Defense of Marriage Act in 1996. It should be repealed and I will vote for its repeal on the Senate floor. I will also oppose any proposal to amend the U.S. Constitution to ban gays and lesbians from marrying. I know how important the issue of equal rights is to the LGBT community. I share your sense of urgency.

Windy City Times, February 11, 2004

ON GENERATIONAL CONFLICT

A lot of the political arguments that we see now are continuations of arguments that took place in the '60s. What I'm seeing out in the country is, particularly in younger generations, wanting to get beyond some of those arguments and saying to themselves, look, the very personal, very vitriolic, deep-seated animosities that were created in that era are over.

Charlie Rose Show, October 19, 2006

When you watch Clinton vs. Gingrich, or Gore vs. Bush, or Kerry vs. Bush, you feel like these are fights that were taking place back in dorm rooms in the '60s.

Sunday Times Magazine, November 5, 2006

I think that older folks hang on too long and stay in the way. I think that if a young person feels they can do a better job than somebody in the next generation, sometimes it's necessary to go ahead and run, and keep in mind that usually folks don't give up power easily. It has to be wrested from them.

Black Collegian, October 2006

ON GLOBAL WARMING

Maybe there are a couple of holdouts in the White House that don't believe in climate change. But there are 10,000 scientists who believe that maybe we should do something about it.

San Francisco Chronicle, October 28, 2006

ON GLOBALIZATION

As the world continues to change and we become more connected to each other, globalization will bring both benefits and disruptions to our lives. But either way, it's here, and it's not going away. We can try to build walls around us, and we can look inward, and we can respond by being frightened and angry about those disruptions. But that's not what we're about.

University of Massachusetts at Boston Commencement Address,
June 2, 2006

ON GUN CONTROL

I believe in keeping guns out of our inner cities, and that our leaders must say so in the face of the gun manufacturer's lobby. But I also believe that when a gangbanger shoots indiscriminately into a crowd because he feels someone disrespected him, we have a problem of morality. Not only do we need to punish that man for his crime, but we need to acknowledge that there's a hole in his heart, one that government programs alone may not be able to repair.

The Audacity of Hope, page 215

ON HEALTH CARE

As progressives, we believe in affordable health care for all Americans, and we're going to make sure that Americans don't have to choose between a health care plan that bankrupts the government and one that bankrupts families. The party won't just throw a few tax breaks at families who can't afford their insurance, but will modernize our health care system and give every family a chance to buy insurance at a price they can afford.

Annual Take Back America Conference, June 14, 2006

The prescription drug bill that was passed by Bush was a fundamentally flawed piece of legislation. We have a bill that's bad for taxpayers and bad for senior citizens. Taxpayers are hit with a half-a-trillion-dollar tab that was originally estimated at three hundred billion. And seniors have a big donut hole in the middle of their benefits. What I would do is say that senior citizens, through the Medicare program, can go and negotiate the best possible price as a consequence of being bulk purchasers.

Illinois Senate Debate, Illinois Radio Network, October 12, 2004

ON HILLARY CLINTON

She has gone through some battles that, in some cases unfairly, have created a perception about her that is different from how I am perceived.

Chicago Tribune, December 15, 2006

I think very highly of Hillary. The more I get to know her, the more I admire her. I think she's the most disciplined—one of the most disciplined people—I've ever met. She's one of the toughest. She's got an extraordinary intelligence. And she's somebody who's in this stuff for the right reasons.

New Yorker, October 30, 2006

I have tremendous respect for Hillary Clinton. She's an outstanding leader in the Democratic Party. She's earned her stripes.

Newsweek, December 25, 2006

I think Hillary is a wonderfully intelligent and capable person. I'm sure that, should she decide to run for president, she will be a formidable candidate.

Face the Nation, March 12, 2006

ON HOMELAND SECURITY

Regarding the inspections of ports, we are currently inspecting only three percent of all incoming cargo. Terrorists could load up a cargo container and drive it straight into the middle of the Loop without significant risk of them being inspected. Our chemical and nuclear plants are still unsecured, despite how vulnerable they are. There are a whole host of domestic priorities that have been neglected by the Bush administration.

Illinois Senate Debate, October 26, 2004

ON IMMIGRATION POLICY

It behooves us to remember that not every single immigrant who came into the United States through Ellis Island had proper documentation. Not every one of our grandparents or great-grandparents would have qualified for legal immigration. But they came here in search of a dream, in search of hope. Americans understand that, and they are willing to give an opportunity to those who are already here, as long as we get serious about making sure that our borders actually mean something. Today's immigrants seek to follow in the same tradition of immigration that has built this country. We do ourselves and them a disservice if we do not recognize the contributions of these individuals. And we fail to protect our Nation if we do not regain control over our immigration system immediately.

Floor Statement on Immigration Reform, April 3, 2006

We're a nation of immigrants. But if those folks are going to live in this country, they have to be put on a pathway to citizenship that involves them paying a fine, making sure that they are at the back of the line and not cutting in front of people who applied legally to come into the country. We've got to have employer sanctions that can actually be enforced. And that's probably the most important thing we can do.

Larry King Live, October 19, 2006

One of the central components of immigration reform is enforcement, and this bill contains a number of important provisions to beef up border security. But that's not enough. Real enforcement also means drying up the pool of jobs that encourages illegal immigration. And that can only happen if employers don't hire illegal workers. Unfortunately, our current employer enforcement system does little to nothing to deter illegal immigrants from finding work. We need an electronic verification system that can effectively detect the use of fraudulent documents, significantly reduce the employment of illegal workers, and give employers the confidence that their workforce is legal.

Floor Statement on the Employment Verification Amendment, May 23, 2006

ON IMPEACHING BUSH

[Someone asked me] shouldn't the president be impeached for lying? Well, with FDR, JFK, and LBJ, we have a pretty long list of presidents who maybe were not entirely forthcoming with intelligence information before they went to war, so I'd be cautious against making legal cases against the administration.

Chicago Tribune, December 5, 2005

ON THE INTERNET

We can't have a situation in which the corporate duopoly dictates the future of the Internet and that's why I'm supporting what is called Net Neutrality. And part of the reason for that is companies like Google and Yahoo might never have gotten started had they not been in a position to easily access the Internet and do so on the same terms as the big corporate companies that were interested in making money on the Internet.

"Network Neutrality" podcast, June 8, 2006

I think the danger of blogs is that we are only talking to ourselves and people who agree with us. That means that over time we are just reinforcing our own preconceptions and we are not opening up to other ideas and other points of view. One of the things I am always trying to figure out is how to get different bloggers and different points of view communicating so it is a conversation and dialogue, not just all of us cheering each other on.

Heightsmom.blogspot.com, June 4, 2006

ON IRAN

Iran is a classic case of something biting us on the ankle, when we assisted in overthrowing the democratically elected regime that was replaced by the Shah.

New Yorker, January 15, 2007

ON IRAQ

There are no good options left in this war.

"A Way Forward in Iraq" speech, November 20, 2006

We're not going to babysit a civil war.

The Today Show, January 11, 2007

I'm not opposed to all wars, I'm opposed to dumb wars. I'm opposed to rash wars. I am opposed to wars that are ideologically driven, and based on power and politics instead of reason.

Charlie Rose Show, October 19, 2006

Our troops can help suppress the violence, but they cannot solve its root causes. And all the troops in the world won't be able to force Shia, Sunni, and Kurd to sit down at a table, resolve their differences, and forge a lasting peace.

Chicago Tribune, November 21, 2006

It is time to give Iraqis their country back. I believe that it remains possible to salvage an acceptable outcome to this long and misguided war. But I have to be honest, it will not be easy.

St. Louis Post-Dispatch, November 20, 2006

We got distracted in Iraq and we ended up pursuing a course that was based on faulty intelligence, fudged numbers, and a shading of the truth, and we are seeing the results.

Larry King Live, October 19, 2006

It's not going to matter how many troops we have there. If the Iraqi people have not taken the responsibility for forming a government that recognizes the importance of all parties being involved—and, most importantly, makes certain that the government apparatus, the security apparatus, is in the hands of nonsectarians—then we are not going to be able to impose order in that country.

Face the Nation, March 12, 2006

We're still mired in a tragic and costly war that should have never been waged.

Barackobama.com

I don't know any military expert who says that a modest increase in troop levels is going to make a big difference. Even if you pursue the logic of increased troop levels, you're going to need one hundred thousand more, one hundred and fifty thousand more, orders of magnitude that we don't possess. Twenty thousand troops is not going to make a difference anymore.

New Yorker, January 15, 2007

The administration has narrowed an entire debate about war into two camps: "cut-and-run" or "stay the course." If you offer any criticism or even mention that we should take a second look at our strategy and change our approach, you are branded "cut-and-run." If you are ready to blindly trust the administration no matter what they do, you are willing to "stay the course."

Chicago Tribune, November 23, 2005

In the end, Iraq is not about one person's legacy, a political campaign, or rigid adherence to an ideology. What is happening in Iraq is about the security of the United States. It is about our men and women in uniform. It is about the future of the Middle East. It is about the world in which our children will live.

Speech to the Chicago Council on Foreign Relations, November 22, 2005

When we establish and send a signal through our troop withdrawals that, in fact, we are not solely responsible for putting Iraq back together again, then we start providing the space for other entities— international community, regional powers, and the Iraqis, most importantly—to join together and start thinking about what's the solution.

Charlie Rose Show, October 19, 2006

The Bush administration has been naive throughout. It was naive to think that we'd be greeted as liberators in Iraq. It's been naive in thinking that somehow this would actually diminish recruitment for terrorism. In fact, it's accelerated it. It's been naive with respect to how difficult it's been to secure the peace, and our troops and our taxpayers are suffering from those errors.

Illinois Senate Debate, October 26, 2004

It's not a great bargain for the next President to take over the mess in Iraq. But there is as much pressure in both the Republican and Democratic camps, because both have genuine concern for the troops and the families and the budget. It won't be good for congressmen of the President's party if we're still spending two billion dollars a week in Iraq in two years.

New Yorker, January 15, 2007

It makes sense for us to begin a phased withdrawal of our troops. I think it is time for us to tell the Iraqis they are responsible for their country and they've got to make a decision about how they want to live together.

Larry King Live, October 19, 2006

I'm not one of those people who cynically believes Bush went in only for the oil.

New York Magazine, October 2, 2006

We absolutely have an obligation to the Iraqi people. That's why I've resisted calls for an immediate withdrawal.

New Yorker, January 15, 2007

Every American wants to see a peaceful and stable Iraq. No American wants to leave behind a security vacuum filled with terrorism, chaos, ethnic cleansing, and genocide. But no American wants a war without end—a war where our goals and strategies drift aimlessly, regardless of the cost in lives or dollars spent, and where we end up with arbitrary, poll-driven troop reductions by the administration—the worst of all possible outcomes.

Speech to the Chicago Council on Foreign Relations, November 22, 2005

ON ISLAM

There are so many different interpretations of Islam as there are so many different interpretations of Christianity, that to somehow fix or define a religion based on one particular reading of the text is a mistake.

Newsweek, September 25, 2006

All of us, particularly religious leaders, have to be mindful that there are a lot of sensitivities out there. Now, the flip side is that there are those in the Muslim community who are looking to take offense and are constantly on the lookout for anything that would indicate that the West is somehow antagonistic toward Islam.

Newsweek, September 25, 2006

ON ISOLATIONISM

We cannot afford isolationism—not only because our work with respect to stabilizing Iraq is not complete, but because our missteps in Iraq have distracted us from the larger threat of terrorism that we face, a threat that we can only meet by working internationally, in cooperation with other countries.

Speech to the Chicago Council on Foreign Relations, November 22, 2005

We cannot afford to be a country of isolationists right now. 9/11 showed us that, try as we might to ignore the rest of the world, our enemies will no longer ignore us.

"A Way Forward in Iraq" speech, November 20, 2006

[The U.S. should] use American moral authority and credibility to help achieve Middle East peace. Our first and immutable commitment must be to the security of Israel, our only true ally in the Middle East and the only democracy. We must be consistent and we must include the EU and the Arab states in pressing for reforms within the Palestinian community.

"Renewal of American Leadership" press release, July 12, 2004

The Bush Administration's failure to be consistently involved in helping Israel achieve peace with the Palestinians has been both wrong for our friendship with Israel, as well as badly damaging to our standing in the Arab world. I do not pretend to have all the answers to this vexing problem, and untangling the issues involved is an appropriate topic for a separate speech. What I can say is this: not only must we be consistent, but we will not succeed unless we have the cooperation of the European Union and the Arab states in pressing for reforms within the Palestinian community.

Speech to the Chicago Council on Foreign Relations, July 12, 2004

ON THE ISSUES

[The] issues are never simple. One thing I'm proud of is that very rarely will you hear me simplify the issues.

MSNBC, September 25, 2006

I really have to make sure that everything I do focuses on the substance and the issues. If I stay focused on that, I'll have my good days and my bad days, but at least I'll always feel I'm on solid ground.

Chicago Tribune, February 24, 2006

A lot of the issues that I see are not an either-or situation. Rather, my perceptions about how we solve problems in health care or education span across a whole range of areas. And I want to try to capture that complexity.

Chicago Tribune, October 26, 2006

I try to describe both sides of the issue, because part of what [*The Audacity of Hope*] is about is trying to figure out how do we build common ground. Ironically, if I get criticized, usually it's because people feel that I take too much care to see all points of view.

All Things Considered, October 19, 2006

ON JOBS

I would focus on improving funding for job-training programs and changing tax codes to give corporations incentives to stay in the country rather than go overseas.

Essence, March 2004

For us to tell the 55-year-old who has been working in a steel plant all his life, to suddenly retrain to become a computer scientist, that's not going to happen. What we can do is we can say, your health care is still going to be available, although you lost your job. We are going to provide you some semblance of retirement security, and we're going to protect the pension rights that you had earned.

Charlie Rose Show, October 19, 2006

We talk a lot about retraining. We don't do it very well, partly because Democrats sometimes are too suspicious of market solutions. The flip side is, sometimes conservatives have a tendency to say it will work out, folks will figure it out. And particularly in rural communities and in small towns across America, they need somebody to link them up with what are the growth jobs, what are the opportunities out there.

Charlie Rose Show, October 19, 2006

Right now, we have a tax code that gives incentives for companies to move offshore. Instead, we must have a tax code that rewards companies that are doing the right thing by investing in American workers and investing in research and development here in the United States. Our government has to be looking out for these people who are working hard everyday trying to make ends meet and right now we've got a set of policies that are not reflective of that.

"Creating Jobs in America" press release, June 21, 2004

ON JOHN McCAIN

I don't think you need a lot of imagination to figure out how they would run that campaign. "We live in dangerous times. Terrorism's looming. We need a battle-tested leader and that's John McCain." I think that's how they would present it.

Chicago Tribune, December 15, 2006

John gets excited sometimes. John's been in the Senate for close to twenty years, he's a war hero, if he wants to vent once in a while, that's not a problem. I think he has good intentions, and both of us want to see a good bill [on lobbying and ethics reform]. I did tell someone I'm going for an Emmy next [after he won a Grammy for Best Spoken Word Album]. It's going to be for Best Actor in a Drama Involving John McCain.

Time, February 13, 2006

People see John McCain as a prima donna. I think of him as a role model.

ON HIS KEYNOTE SPEECH AT THE 2004 DEMOCRATIC CONVENTION

I like writing my own stuff. So I made a rare intelligent decision to start writing immediately after I was asked to deliver the speech. And so I actually had a draft completed before it was publicly announced, which was helpful, because if I'd known it was such a big deal, I might have gotten nervous and gotten writer's block.

I am not a propagandist. That's not my job. My job and my intent in delivering a speech like this is I'm trying to speak truthfully as I can about what I see out there. If I'm restricted or prescribed in my statements because the media or Republicans—or Democrats—are going to interpret what I say through the Republican frame, I'm not going to spend a lot of time saying very much.

Streetprophets.com, January 16, 2007

ON HIS LACK OF EXPERIENCE

The test of leadership in my mind is not going to be what's on a paper resume.

Chicago Tribune, December 15, 2006

I am new enough on the political scene that I serve as a blank screen on which people of vastly different political stripes project their own views. As such, I am bound to disappoint some, if not all, of them.

The Times of London, October 26, 2006

I think that experience question would be answered during the course of the campaign. Either at the end of that campaign, people would say, "He looked good on paper but the guy was kind of way too green," or at the end of the campaign they say, "He's run a really strong campaign and we think he's got something to say and we think he could lead us."

Chicago Tribune, December 15, 2006

It is entirely legitimate for people to look at the body of my experience and ask the tough questions and put us through the process. If I decide to run at the end of that process, people will know me pretty well.

Milwaukee Journal Sentinel, December 11, 2006

Dick Cheney and Donald Rumsfeld have an awful lot of experience.

Vanity Fair, February 2007

ON HIS MARRIAGE

She [Michelle] is the smartest, toughest, funniest best friend that I could ever hope for, and she's always had my back. Whatever decision we make, we'll make together.

Washington Post, December 11, 2006

Barack didn't pledge riches, only a life that would be interesting. On that promise he delivered.

Michelle Obama in the *Sunday Times Magazine*, November 5, 2006

It is important that when I'm home to make sure that I'm present. I still forget stuff. As Michelle likes to say, "You are a good man, but you are still a man." I leave my socks around. I'll hang my pants on the door. She lets me know when I'm not acting right. After 14 years, she's trained me reasonably well.

Ebony, February 2007

She is my life partner and we make decisions together. She doesn't have a real hankering to be in the public eye or be in politics, but she has a wonderful sense of what good, solid, Midwestern, ordinary folks are thinking.

Larry King Live, October 19, 2006

She cares more about whether I'm a good father and a good husband than she does about whether I'm a U.S. senator. As she likes to say, she would be my Number 1 political supporter—she'd make calls and raise money—if I were her neighbor. She would be leading the bandwagon for me to run for President if I was married to somebody else.

New Yorker, October 30, 2006

My wife is not impressed by what's said about me in the press. She's impressed by whether I take out the garbage, take the kids to the park.

Essence, October 2006

My wife just tells me to not screw it up.

National Review, July 27, 2004

ON THE MEDIA

One of the things that I'm always battling—and I've only been on the national stage for a couple of years now—is that tendency to edit yourself so much that, at a certain point, you stop sounding like a regular person and you start taking on the persona of those bad politicians in TV movies.

Talk of the Nation, November 2, 2006

Everybody has got an ax to grind when it comes to the press. My attitude is, let the press do its job.

Hannity & Colmes, June 28, 2006

I'm surprised by the media interest in me and my candidacy. It's a little over the top, and I am not somebody who spends a lot of time reading my own press clippings.

USA Today, July 27, 2004

You're in the public eye, and people ask you the same questions over and over again, and you start giving rote answers. You become almost a caricature of yourself.

San Francisco Chronicle, October 26, 2006

I've got a wife who knocks me down a peg anytime I start believing what they're writing about me is true.

Toronto Star, October 26, 2006

ON THE MIDDLE EAST

Let's fight to make sure our so-called allies in the Middle East, the Saudis and the Egyptians, stop oppressing their own people, and suppressing dissent, and tolerating corruption and inequality, and mismanaging their economies so that their youth grow up without education, without prospects, without hope, the ready recruits of terrorist cells.

Speech at anti-Iraq War rally in Chicago, October 26, 2002

We depend on some of the most politically volatile countries in the Middle East and elsewhere to fuel our energy needs. It doesn't matter if they're budding democracies, despotic regimes with nuclear intentions, or havens for the *madrassas* that plant the seeds of terror in young minds. They get our money because we need their oil.

Crain's Chicago Business, September 4, 2006

ON THE MILITARY

Operations in Iraq and Afghanistan and the war on terrorism have reduced the pace of military transformation and have revealed our lack of preparation for defensive and stability operations. This administration has overextended our military.

Speech to the Chicago Council on Foreign Relations, July 12, 2004

ON MIXING POLITICS AND RELIGION

I don't think it's healthy for public figures to wear religion on their sleeve as a means to insulate themselves from criticism or dialogue with people who disagree with them.

Chicago Sun-Times, April 5, 2004

Those who are religious have to translate their religious-motivated agenda into universal terms that are amenable to reason. It is not sufficient if you are against gay marriage or against abortion to simply say God told me so, and then expect other people to feel, well, okay, if God is talking to you, I guess we have got to go along.

Charlie Rose Show, October 19, 2006

Today, faith drives so much of our politics, that I thought if you don't talk about it, you are missing a whole big part of what is going on politically.

Chicago Tribune, October 26, 2004

I don't want the Democrats to suddenly pretend like they found religion if they haven't.

All Things Considered, March 10, 2005

The world will [eventually] look more like Brazil, with its racial mix. America is getting more complex. The color line in America being black and white is out the window. That does break down barriers.

Crisis, October 1995

ON HIS MULTIRACIAL HERITAGE

The starting premise for me that my mother instilled in me, and my father inadvertently instilled, was that everybody was the same.

Speech at the Aspen Institute, July 2, 2005

I've always been clear that I'm rooted in the African-American community but not limited to it.

The Washington Post, July 27, 2004

I'm certainly black enough to have trouble catching a cab in New York City.

Tavis Smiley Show, March 29, 2004

There were elements within the African-American community who might have suggested, "Well he's from Hyde Park or he went to Harvard or he was born in Hawaii so he might not be black enough." I had to make a name for myself, but having made that name, people take me at face value and don't hoist onto me a set of expectations or understandings based on something my parents did.

Chicago Tribune, June 26, 2005

The African-American community is, by definition, a hybrid culture. We draw on all these different elements. But you know, as I've grown up in the United States, I have been identified as an African-American. I'm comfortable with that identification. I'm rooted in that culture and draw inspiration from that tradition.

All Things Considered, July 27, 2004

ON HIS NAME

I was told, people will remember your name and won't like it. You can have one African name, but not two. You can be Barack Smith or Joe Obama—but not Barack Obama.

Live Your Best Life, Oprah Winfrey, page 292

Some people call me Alabama.

U.S. News & World Report, August 2, 2004

ON NATIONAL SECURITY

What I think should be a national security framework that hearkens back to what we did right after World War II, and Truman and Acheson and George Marshall helped to craft a policy of containment, engagement with other countries, creating NATO, creating strong alliances, creating a set of international rules of the road that all of us could abide by.

Larry King Live, October 19, 2006

From a national-security posture, there's not a better thing we could do—for example, dealing with proliferation issues in Iran—than to drive the price of oil down to twenty-five bucks a barrel. It's the single biggest thing we could do to effectuate change and cut the legs out of some of the fundamentalist impulses in the Middle East.

New Yorker, October 30, 2006

Every democracy is tested when it is faced with a serious threat. As a nation, we have to find the right balance between privacy and security, between executive authority to face threats and uncontrolled power. What protects us, and what distinguishes us, are the procedures we put in place to protect that balance, namely judicial warrants and congressional review. These aren't arbitrary ideas. These are the concrete safeguards that make sure that surveillance hasn't gone too far.

Speech on the confirmation of Michael Hayden, May 25, 2006

ON NORTH KOREA

Just because they're state actors doesn't mean they might not act irrationally. We can't gauge their decision-making process accurately, partly because our intelligence capabilities have been entirely inadequate to the task, and partly due to the nature of the regimes. Whatever you want to say about the Soviets, they were essentially conservative. The North Korean regime is driven more by ideology and fantasy.

New Yorker, January 15, 2007

[We should] address the threat posed by North Korea. By refusing to negotiate with North Korea for three and half years, experts believe that North Korea may now be close to having six to eight nuclear weapons. We must immediately insist on complete and verifiable elimination of North Korea's nuclear capability, engage in Six-Party bilateral talks, and facilitate a reform agenda that is broader than denuclearization to address humanitarian concerns.

"Renewal of American Leadership" press release, July 12, 2004

ON NUCLEAR WEAPONS

Let's fight to make sure that the U.N. inspectors can do their work, and that we vigorously enforce a non-proliferation treaty, and that former enemies and current allies like Russia safeguard and ultimately eliminate their stores of nuclear material, and that nations like Pakistan and India never use the terrible weapons already in their possession, and that the arms merchants in our own country stop feeding the countless wars that rage across the globe.

Speech at anti-Iraq War rally in Chicago, October 26, 2002

ON HIS PERSONAL INTEGRITY

I'm very proud of how I've conducted myself during the entire time I've been in public service. My hope would be that people come away saying, "He's not perfect, but he owns up to his mistakes and tries to correct them as quickly as possible."

Washington Post, December 17, 2006

I got a free pass because I wasn't subjected to a bunch of negative ads. And nobody thought I was going to win. So I basically got into the habit of pretty much saying what I thought. And it worked for me. So I figured I might as well keep on doing it.

New York Magazine, October 2, 2006

At some level, your individual salvation depends on collective salvation. It's only when you hitch yourself up to something bigger than yourself that you're going to realize your true potential, and the world will benefit from that potential.

Diverse: Issues in Higher Education, August 10, 2006

When I hear "With malice toward none, with charity toward all" being quoted, and all we have around here is malice toward all and charity toward none, it gets me frustrated. There are risks in including that kind of approach in a speech like that because it's a feel-good event, but one of the things that I'm trying to be mindful of is not starting to get so comfortable or risk-averse that I end up sounding like everyone else.

Chicago Tribune, June 26, 2005

You should always assume that when I cast a vote or make a state-ment it is because it is what I believe in. The thing that bothers me is the assumption that if I make a judgment that's different from yours, then it must mean I am less progressive or my goals are different, meaning I must be not really committed to helping people.

The Nation, June 26, 2006

ON HIS PERSONAL STRENGTHS

I can walk into a room, whether they're black, white, rural, urban, red state, blue state, and after thirty minutes, engage them in a con-versation where they say, a lot of what this guy is saying makes sense.

Charlie Rose Show, October 19, 2006

And if you talk to my wife, she'll tell you that there are times when I do not put aside childish things; when I continually struggle to rise above the selfish or the petty or the small.

Northwestern University Commencement Address, June 16, 2006

I like to think I have a message that's useful, I like to think that I can contribute, otherwise I wouldn't have written [*The Audacity of Hope*]. There's the question of whether I am the right messenger for whatever message that is. And that's not clear as well, because, like anybody in politics, I've got strengths and I've got weaknesses, both politically and substantively.

New Yorker, October 30, 2006

I'm a self-confessed policy wonk.

Chicago Tribune, March 20, 2005

I probably always feel on some level I can persuade anybody I talk to.

Time, February 20, 2006

I feel confident that if you put me in a room with anybody—black, white, Hispanic, Republican, Democrat—give me half an hour and I will walk out with the votes of most of the folks. I don't feel constrained by race, geography, or background in terms of making a connection with people.

People Weekly, December 25, 2006

The fact that I conjugate my verbs and speak in a typical Midwestern newscaster voice, there's no doubt this helps ease communication between myself and white audiences. And there's no doubt that when I'm with a black audience, I slip into a slightly different dialect. I don't feel the need to talk in a certain way before a white audience. And I don't feel the need to speak a certain way in front of a black audience. There's a level of self-consciousness about these issues the previous generation had to negotiate that I don't feel I have to.

New York Magazine, October 2, 2006

I don't think humility is contradictory with ambition. I feel very humble about what I don't know. But I'm plain ambitious in terms of wanting to actually deliver some benefit for the people of Illinois.

Chicago Tribune, March 20, 2005

I'm comfortable in my own skin.

Rolling Stone, December 30, 2004

ON HIS POLITICAL AGENDA

I want to make real the American ideal that every child in this country has a shot at life. Right now, that's not true.

Live Your Best Life, Oprah Winfrey, page 293

Over the next six years, there will be occasions where people will be surprised by my positions. I won't be as easy to categorize as many people expect.

Chicago Tribune, March 20, 2005

My street cred as a progressive is not something I worry too much about. People can look at the ten years that I've been in politics and pull the legislation I've passed and look at my votes and get a pretty good sense of what my values are and where I'm coming from. That's not something I worry about.

Time, February 13, 2006

My job is to inspire people to take ownership of this country. Politics is not a business. It's a mission. It's about making people's lives better.

Essence, March 2004

Since the founding, the American political tradition has been reformist, not revolutionary. What that means is that for a political leader to get things done, he or she ideally should be ahead of the curve, but not too far ahead. I want to push the envelope but make sure I have enough folks with me that I'm not rendered politically impotent.

Harper's, November 2006

ON POLITICAL CAMPAIGNING

I don't know about you, but the war against terrorism isn't supposed to crop up just between September and November in even-numbered years. That seems to be the pattern.

Salon, September 18, 2006

I wouldn't run if I didn't think I could win.

Chicago Tribune, December 15, 2006

We have a long and rigorous election process and, if I ever did decide to run [for President], I'm confident that I'd be run through the paces pretty good.

Sunday Times Magazine, November 5, 2006

The Democrats will continue to squabble. You've got at least eight Democrats running for the presidency. It means all of them have an incentive not to unify around a strategy, but to distinguish themselves, to break out of the pack. So I'd say we're gonna have some silly season going on.

New York Magazine, October 2, 2006

I'm a public figure, and I wouldn't have gone into public life if I wasn't interested in shaping the debate and moving it forward.

New Yorker, October 30, 2006

When I look at what happened in my race, the ability of the Internet to spread the word about a campaign for a candidate who wasn't that well known was absolutely critical.

Heightsmom.blogspot.com, June 4, 2006

ON HIS POLITICAL CAREER

I think what's worked for me has been the capacity to stay true to a set of progressive values but to be eclectic in terms of the tools to achieve those progressive values. To not be orthodox. To be willing to get good ideas from all quarters.

Washington Post, December 11, 2006

I wasn't one of these folks who at the age of five said to myself, "I'm going to be a U.S. senator." The motivation for my work has been more rooted in the need to live up to certain values that my mother instilled in me, and to figure out how you reconcile those values with a world that is broken apart by class and race and nationality. And so I guess I have on occasions had to push myself or I've been pushed into service, not always because I thought it was fun or that it was preferable to sitting down and watching a ball game, but because I felt it was necessary.

Men's Vogue, Fall 2006

My job is not to represent Washington to you, but to represent you to Washington.

Oprah Winfrey Show, October 18, 2006

The reason I'm involved in politics right now is not because I wanted to be JFK; it's because of the civil rights movement. And I think about all those nameless women marching for freedom, not taking the bus when they come home from a hard day's work doing somebody else's laundry. To me, that embodies the best of the American spirit, and that's the standard that I measure myself by.

All Things Considered, July 27, 2004

I am under no illusion that all people throughout the state of Illinois agree with me on every single position.

Election Night Speech, November 2, 2004

ON POLITICAL PARTIES

The single biggest gap in party affiliation among white Americans today is not between men and women, or those who reside in so-called red states and those who reside in blue, but between those who attend church regularly and those who don't.

Call to Renewal Keynote Address, June 28, 2006

One party seems to be defending a moribund status quo, and the other is defending an oligarchy. It's not a very attractive choice.

Newsweek, December 27, 2004

Republicans will have to recognize our collective responsibilities, even as Democrats recognize that we have to do more than just defend old programs.

Knox College Commencement Address, June 4, 2005

ON A POLITICIAN'S PAST

I'm very cautious about attributing a lot of weight to statements that were made twenty or thirty years ago. I don't think it is automatically indicative of what he thinks now.

Chicago Tribune, December 5, 2005

ON POLITICS

What you just get a sense of is that there is a political transition that is going to happen nationally, where people try to break out of some of the conservative-liberal sharp divisions.

Newsweek, September 25, 2006

Our politics at its best involves us recognizing ourselves in each other. And our politics at its worst are when we see immigrants or women or blacks or gays or Mexicans as somehow separate, apart from us.

Chicago Tribune, October 26, 2006

If people are paying attention, then we get good government and good leadership. And when we get lazy as a democracy and civically start taking shortcuts, then it results in bad government and politics.

Newsweek, September 25, 2006

The biggest problem in politics is the fear of loss. It's a very public thing, which most people don't have to go through.

New Yorker, October 30, 2006

If you make political discourse sufficiently negative, more people will become cynical and stop paying attention. That leaves more space for special interests to pursue their agendas, and that's how we end up with drug companies making drug policy, energy companies making energy policy, and multinationals making trade policy.

New Yorker, May 31, 2004

It's not the magnitude of our problems that concerns me the most. It's the smallness of our politics. America's faced big problems before. But today, our leaders in Washington seem incapable of working together in a practical, common sense way. Politics has become so bitter and partisan, so gummed up by money and influence, that we can't tackle the big problems that demand solutions.

Barackobama.com, January 16, 2007

You get a sense that some of my colleagues just feel trapped by the rigidity and the lockstep nature of party politics in Washington. A couple of senators have joked about how their wrists are getting stiff because they were having to vote "no" on everything.

Chicago Tribune, March 20, 2005

What we have now is a surplus amount of conflict that is manufactured. It's manufactured in television ads, it's manufactured in terms of how the parties portray each other. There doesn't seem to be any break from the perpetual campaign. And so we never sit down and actually govern.

Charlie Rose Show, October 19, 2006

The most gratifying feeling in politics is when you hit that sweet spot where everybody concludes that the law that we've just passed works and is going to make things better, and everybody across party lines has to confess that we're probably better off with this thing than not.

New Yorker, October 30, 2006

ON HIS POPULARITY

It's always hard to stand outside yourself and know what it is that people are reacting to. Some of it is just dumb luck.

Newsweek, September 25, 2006

I would not be here had it not been for 1984, or for 1988. If I'm on the cover of *Ebony*, it's not because of me. It's because a whole bunch of folks did the work to put me there.

The Sunday Times, January 14, 2007

I have always been suspicious of our celebrity culture. And now I find myself in this odd position where I am a part of it, and to some degree a beneficiary of it. We cycle through the new and the novel, and stack story after story on top of individuals, until we lose track of who we're talking about. And if you get absorbed in that, you lose track of who you're talking about.

New Yorker, October 30, 2006

Andy Warhol said we all get our fifteen minutes of fame. I've already had an hour and a half. I'm so overexposed, I'm making Paris Hilton look like a recluse.

Sunday Times Magazine, November 5, 2006

It's flattering to get a lot of attention, although I must say it is baffling. I think to some extent I've become a shorthand or symbol or stand-in for a spirit that the last election in New Hampshire represented. It's a spirit that says we are looking for something different, we want something new.

Irish Times, December 12, 2006

There's this weird confluence of events that's making all this possible. But my experience in these kinds of things is that what comes up must come down.

Washington Post, July 27, 2004

Given all the hype surrounding my election, I hope people have gotten a sense that I am here to do work and not just chase cameras. The collateral benefit is that people really like me. I'm not some prima donna.

Chicago Tribune, March 20, 2005

I think there is a great hunger for change in the country, and not just policy change. What I also think they are looking for is change in tone and a return to some notion of the common good and some sense of cooperation, of pragmatism over ideology. I'm a stand-in for that right now.

U.S. News & World Report, January 8, 2007

I'm the flavor of the month. This is a celebrity culture, and that culture has to be fed.

San Francisco Chronicle, October 26, 2006

I've got a celebrity that's undeserved and a little overgrown relative to the actual power that I have in this city.

All Things Considered, March 10, 2005

ON PORK-BARREL SPENDING

Pork is in the eye of the beholder. The recipients don't tend to think it's pork, especially if it's a great public-works project.

Harper's, November 2006

ON THE PRESIDENCY

That's the power of the presidency that I don't see used enough. The capacity to explain to the American people in very prosaic, straightforward terms: here are the choices we have. The biggest problem we have in our politics—and our campaigns press this upon candidates—is to lie about the choices that have to be made. And to obfuscate and to fudge. And so by the time the person arrives, people are already set up for disappointment.

New Yorker, October 30, 2006

I'm not sure anyone is ready to be president before they're president.

Meet the Press, October 22, 2006

America is ready to turn the page. America is ready for a new set of challenges. This is our time. A new generation is prepared to lead.

Washington Post, December 11, 2006

People who are ready are folks who go into it understanding the gravity of their work, and are able to combine vision and judgment. Having knowledge is important. I'm one of those folks—I wouldn't probably fit in with the administration—who actually thinks that being informed is a good basis for policy.

New Yorker, October 30, 2006

My attitude about something like the presidency is that you don't want to just be the president. You want to change the country. You want to make a unique contribution. You want to be a great president.

Men's Vogue, Fall 2006

ON PRESIDENT GEORGE W. BUSH

We all remember that George Bush said in the 2000 campaign that he was against nation-building. We just didn't know he was talking about this one.

Speech, June 14, 2006

I don't think that George Bush is a bad man. [Republicans] just believe in different things.

New York Times, September 18, 2006

I find him actually a decent person. He is an engaging person.

Charlie Rose Show, October 19, 2006

Straight answers to critical questions. That's what we don't have right now.

Washington Post, November 23, 2005

My impression is that one of the president's strengths is he's extremely sincere. And I think that he genuinely feels like he's doing the right thing. I don't think he sees hypocrisy in his actions. I think, in his mind, there's some consistency there.

All Things Considered, March 10, 2005

It is way too simplistic just to say this administration doesn't care about black people. I think it is entirely accurate to say that this administration's policies don't take into account the plight of poor people in poor communities and this is a tragic reflection of that indifference, but I also have to say that it's an indifference that is not entirely partisan.

Chicago Tribune, September 11, 2005

This has been the most ideological administration in my lifetime, even more so than the Reagan administration. The Reagan administration, despite the rhetoric, could be pragmatic.

U.S. News & World Report, January 8, 2007

Now, let me say this: I don't think that George Bush is a bad man. I think he loves his country. I don't think this administration is full of stupid people, I think there are a lot of smart folks in there. The problem isn't that their philosophy isn't working the way it's supposed to, it's that it is. It's that it's doing exactly what it's supposed to do.

Speech, June 14, 2006

This has been probably the most ideologically driven administration in my memory. And I don't know how far I'd have to go back to find one, a combination of a House, Senate, and White House, that has been so obstinate in resisting facts, dissenting opinions, compromise. Everything is based on a set of preconceived notions that ignore whatever reality and information comes at them. I think that this administration has done great damage to this country.

New Yorker, October 30, 2006

We have an administration that believes that the government's role is to protect the powerful from the powerless.

New Yorker, May 31, 2004

For too long now, this can-do spirit has been stifled by a can't-do government that seems to think it has no role in solving great national challenges or rallying a country to a cause.

"Securing Our Energy Future" speech, September 15, 2005

[The president] could take the politics out of Iraq once and for all if he would simply go on television and say to the American people, "Yes, we made mistakes." Imagine if he did that, how it would transform the politics of our country.

Chicago Tribune, November 23, 2005

I think Bush was sincere and is sincere about his desire to maintain a strong America, but there was a single-mindedness to this process that has led our country into a very difficult position. It's a consequence of that single-mindedness that we did not create the kind of international framework that would have allowed success once we decided to go in. I think that this administration is sincere but I think it's misguided.

Meet the Press, July 25, 2004

ON THE PRESIDENT HE'D BE

What I at least think about is, whether through luck or happenstance or serendipity or convergences between my biography and events, do I have a particular ability to bring the country together around a pragmatic, common-sense agenda for change that probably has a generational element to it as well?

Chicago Tribune, December 15, 2006

I'd want to be a really great president. And then I'd worry about all the other stuff. Because there are a lot of mediocre or poor presidents.

New York Magazine, October 2, 2006

ON PRIVACY

Americans fought a Revolution in part over the right to be free from unreasonable searches, to ensure that our government couldn't come knocking in the middle of the night for no reason. We need to find a way forward to make sure that we can stop terrorists while protecting the privacy, and liberty, of innocent Americans.

Speech on the confirmation of Michael Hayden, May 25, 2006

ON RACE

[Non-white candidates have] a higher threshold in establishing themselves with voters.

Milwaukee Journal Sentinel, December 11, 2006

You don't vote for somebody because of what they look like. You vote for what they stand for.

Irish Times, November 4, 2006

The problem is not that things haven't gotten better. The problem is that they're not good enough, and we still have a lot of work to do.

Talk of the Nation, November 2, 2006

I'm not somebody who uses race to score political points—quite the opposite. I would hope that it wouldn't just be something that I would do because I'm black, I would hope that any senator in my position would do the same thing.

Chicago Tribune, June 26, 2005

[Living in Indonesia] made me realize that racism was an extension of other abuses of power. Living there you learned that people can find excuses other than race to oppress each other.

Crisis, October 1995

It was only three or four years ago where if I was standing outside of a restaurant waiting for my car, people would toss me the keys.

Charlie Rose Show, October 19, 2006

I don't want people to pretend I'm not black or that it's somehow not relevant.

Sunday Times Magazine, November 5, 2006

The issue of race now has more to do with wealth and class. That isn't to say there's no discrimination or bias. But I think that if people think you can help them, whether it's in business or politics, they can look beyond color.

Essence, October 2006

Race is a continuing and enormous factor in American life. Always has been. It's sort of the fundamental stain on American life. What is also true is usually American people are more decent than a lot of folks give them credit for. Even when conflicts arise, you sometimes get the sense that they're busy, they're tired, they're stressed.

Who's Afraid of a Large Black Man? Charles Barkley, page 19

ON RELIGION

When we ignore the debate about what it means to be a good Christian or Muslim or Jew; when we discuss religion only in the negative sense of where or how it should not be practiced, rather than in the positive sense of what it tells us about our obligations towards one another, others will fill the vacuum, those with the most insular views of faith, or those who cynically use religion to justify partisan ends.

Call to Renewal Keynote Address, June 28, 2006

At a time when image all too often trumps substance, when our politics all too often feeds rather than bridges division, when the prospects of a poor youth rising out of poverty seem of no consequence to the powerful and when we evoke our common God to condemn those who do not think as we do, rather than to seek God's mercy for our own lack of understanding—at such a time it is helpful to remember this man who was the real thing.

Chicago Tribune, June 26, 2005

I didn't grow up in a religious household. My mother, who was an anthropologist, would take me to church once in a while, and then she would take me to the Buddhist monastery, and then she'd take me to a mosque. Her attitude was religion was fascinating and an expression of human attempts to understand the mysteries of life.

Charlie Rose Show, October 19, 2006

I said if we were supposed to be perfect, we'd all be in trouble. So we rely on God's mercy and grace to get us through.

Chicago Tribune, March 20, 2005

I see faith as more than just a comfort to the weary or a hedge against death. It is an active, palpable agent in the world. It is a source of hope.

Chicago Tribune, June 29, 2006

I think we've got to admit the possibility that we are not always right, that our particular faith may not have all the monopoly on truth, and we've got to be able to listen to other people. You know I think one of the trends we are seeing right now, and which I think is causing so much political grief both domestically and internationally, is that absolutism has become sort of the flavor of the day.

Newsweek, September 25, 2006

ON REPUBLICANS

I think it's great that the Republican Party has discovered black people.

Irish Times, November 4, 2006

The reason they don't believe government has a role in solving national problems is because they think government is the problem.

Speech, June 14, 2006

ON THE ROLE OF GOVERNMENT

My instinct is that the current generation is more interested in smart government. If the market solution works, let's go with the market solution. If a solution requires government intervention, let's do that. But let's look at what are the practical outcomes.

Meet the Press, October 22, 2006

There's a long history of believing that anything government touches is somehow Socialist. I don't understand the view. Because when I drive on the Interstate highway system—we're going to have the Highway Reauthorization this year—nobody says, "You know what? That's your highway, go fix it." I mean, we don't do a fundraiser to patch up the roads.

News conference at National Press Club, April 26, 2005

There's a component of individual responsibility in individual success, but society has a responsibility to give people the tools they need to succeed.

USA Today, July 27, 2004

They're telling us we're better off if we dismantle government. It's called the Ownership Society in Washington. But in our past there has been another term for it—Social Darwinism—every man or women for him or herself. But there's just one problem. It doesn't work. It ignores the fact that it has been government research and investment that has allowed all of us to prosper. And it has been the ability of working men and women to join together in unions that has allowed our rising tide to lift every boat.

Speech at AFSCME National Convention, August 7, 2006

So many of our policy arguments are structured as either/or arguments, and I find this extraordinarily frustrating. You know, the notion that either you have got big government bureaucracies and command and control, or you're just hands off and whatever the market wants to do, let them do it.

Charlie Rose Show, October 19, 2006

They would tell me we don't expect our government to solve all our problems. We know that we have to teach all our own children initiative and self-respect and a sense of family and faith and community. But what we also know is that government can help provide us with the basic tools we need to live out the American dream.

Election Night Speech, November 2, 2004

ON RURAL ISSUES

Our rural communities are the backbone of Illinois. Yet, factories have closed, jobs have disappeared, and homes and farms have been foreclosed upon. Effective federal programs are necessary to protect the rural economy.

ObamaForIllinois.com, May 2, 2004

ON SADDAM HUSSEIN

Now let me be clear: I suffer no illusions about Saddam Hussein. He is a brutal man. A ruthless man. A man who butchers his own people to secure his own power. The world, and the Iraqi people, would be better off without him. But I also know that Saddam poses no imminent and direct threat to the United States, or to his neighbors, and that in concert with the international community he can be contained until, in the way of all petty dictators, he falls away into the dustbin of history.

Speech at anti-Iraq War rally in Chicago, October 26, 2002

ON THE SENATE

When you're voting on a bill, half the time the bill is a hodgepodge— maybe more than half the time—of different things, some good and some bad. And oftentimes, particularly when you're in the minority party, you're voting on legislation that you had no input in that strikes compromises that you yourself would not want to strike.

Talk of the Nation, November 2, 2006

The budget process in particular is so undisciplined, and so opaque, that it is very difficult for any senator to know what they're voting on when it comes to budgetary matters at any given time. You've got this big monster bill. And those who control that process are able to slip in and massage and work on whatever they want.

New Yorker, October 30, 2006

There's a famous saying that every United States senator wakes up in the morning, looks in the mirror and looks at a future president. It's one of the congenital defects of serving in the United States Senate.

Larry King Live, October 19, 2006

Each time I walk onto the Senate floor, I'm reminded of the history, for good and for ill, that has been made there.

Knox College Commencement Address, June 4, 2005

Anybody who knows the U.S. Senate, knows that to be the only African American in that body is a tremendous responsibility.

Barackobama.com

The fact that I am—deservedly or not—a celebrity plays more of a role in the Senate leadership being interested in me participating in these events than the fact that I'm African-American. I receive a lot of attention. That is one form of currency in politics, and I think that people have been interested in seeing how that celebrity can help bring focus to the issues they were trying to highlight.

Chicago Tribune, June 26, 2005

The Senate is a clubby institution. Individual senators here, I have the utmost respect for and I think they do an excellent job for their constituents. But they don't really like people intruding on Senate business, and part of what we need right now is some sunshine as a disinfectant in Washington.

Speech on Lobbying and Ethics Reform, February 9, 2006

One of the toughest things about being a senator is most of the time you can't punch the box that says "none of the above."

Charlie Rose Show, October 19, 2006

The amount of publicity I have received means that I've got to be more sensitive in some ways to not step on my colleagues.

The Nation, June 26, 2006

When you think of the history of the Senate, what is striking is the degree to which this institution has single-handedly blocked the progress of African-Americans for much of our history. That's a sad testament to our institution. It's a stain on the institution. I don't perceive now that the battles that are going on in the Senate revolve around race as much as they revolve around economics.

Chicago Tribune, June 26, 2005

I'm pleasantly surprised at how much I got done. I feel like we had some concrete accomplishments. I'm surprised at the lack of deliberation in the world's greatest deliberative body. We have press releases passing in the night and floor statements nobody is listening to. And the fact that things move so slow. My last year in the Illinois Senate, I passed 26 bills in a year.

Time, February 13, 2006

Given the complexity of the issues that are involved, you can spend six years here being very busy and not get anything done.

All Things Considered, March 10, 2005

ON THE SEPARATION OF CHURCH AND STATE

Those of us who are seeking to police that line don't have to be absolutist about it. Not every mention of God in a public place oppresses folks.

Charlie Rose Show, October 19, 2006

ON SPREADING DEMOCRACY

The United States should be more modest in our belief that we can impose democracy on a country through military force.

St. Louis Post-Dispatch, November 20, 2006

ON STEM CELL RESEARCH

This bill affects diseases that attack Americans regardless of their gender, age, economic status, ethnicity, race, or political affiliation. This is about a commitment to medical research under strict federal guidelines. I call on leaders in Illinois and President Bush in Washington to stop playing politics on this critical issue and expand the current policy on embryonic stem cell research so that we can begin finding the cures of tomorrow today.

Stem Cell Research Bill press release, June 16, 2004

ON TERRORISM

We must always reserve the right to strike unilaterally at terrorists wherever they may exist.

"A Way Forward in Iraq" speech, November 20, 2006

Our battle against radical Islamist terrorism will not be altered overnight, stability in the Middle East must be part of our strategy to defeat terrorism, military power is a key part of our national security, and our strategy cannot be poll driven.

Speech to the Chicago Council on Foreign Relations, November 22, 2005

It makes more sense for us to focus on those terrorists who are active where we have evidence that in fact these countries are being used as staging grounds that would potentially cause us eminent harm, and then we go in. The U.S. has to reserve all military options in facing such an imminent threat, but we have to do it wisely.

Illinois Senate Debate, Illinois Radio Network, October 12, 2004

Let's finish the fight with Bin Laden and al-Qaeda, through effective, coordinated intelligence, and a shutting down of the financial networks that support terrorism, and a homeland security program that involves more than color-coded warnings.

Speech at anti-Iraq War rally in Chicago, October 26, 2002

ON VETERANS

When you look at the Department for Veterans Affairs, I think it is unconscionable for us to stand by our troops and hoist the flag and suggest how patriotic we are at the same time as the veterans' budget is being effectively cut.

All Things Considered, March 10, 2005

One of the things that I'm going to be monitoring very closely is how are we treating the 100,000 plus veterans who are coming home, and to make sure the V.A. has the capacity to provide transition services for veterans who are leaving the service and reentering civilian life, particularly National Guardsmen and Reservists who perhaps did not expect to be fighting in a place like Iraq. It turns out that if you catch a veteran and provide them good services on the way out, they are much less likely to suffer Post-traumatic Stress Disorder and can make the adjustment.

"Honoring Our Commitment to Veterans" podcast, May 18, 2006

ON VOTER ID CARDS

Why shouldn't we require people to have a voter ID card when they vote? Don't we want to make sure voters are who they claim to be? And shouldn't we make sure non-citizens are casting ballots to change the outcome of elections? There are two problems: number one, there's no proof that there's any significant problem with voter fraud in the fifty states. There certainly is none showing that non-citizens are rushing to try to vote: this is a solution in search of a problem. Second is that historically disenfranchised groups—minorities, the poor, the elderly, and the disabled—are most affected by photo ID laws.

Floor Statement on requiring a photo ID to vote, May 24, 2006

ON WAR

The consequences of war are dire, the sacrifices immeasurable. We may have occasion in our lifetime to once again rise up in defense of our freedom, and pay the wages of war. But we ought not—we will not—travel down that hellish path blindly. Nor should we allow those who would march off and pay the ultimate sacrifice, who would prove the full measure of devotion with their blood, to make such an awful sacrifice in vain.

Speech at anti-Iraq War rally in Chicago, October 26, 2002

There is no more profound decision that we can make than the decision to send this nation's youth to war, and that we have a moral obligation not only to send them for good reasons, but to constantly examine, based on the best information and judgment available, in what manner, and for what purpose, and for how long we keep them in harm's way.

Speech to the Chicago Council on Foreign Relations, November 22, 2005

ON THE WAR ON TERROR

The war on terror has to be vigorously fought.

Illinois Senate Debate, Illinois Radio Network, October 12, 2004

Why do we make our economy hostage to some of the most hostile nations on Earth? Why would we spend $800 million a day on countries that do not have our best interest at heart and fund both sides of the war on terror?

San Francisco Chronicle, October 28, 2006

The war against international terrorism has pitted us against a new kind of enemy that wages terror in new and unconventional ways. At home, fighting that enemy won't require us to build the massive war machine that Franklin Roosevelt called for so many years ago, but it will require us to harness our own renewable forms of energy so that oil can never be used as a weapon against America.

Speech at the Governor's Ethanol Coalition, February 28, 2006

Where the stakes are the highest in the war on terror, we cannot possibly succeed without extraordinary international cooperation. Effective international police actions require the highest degree of intelligence sharing, planning, and collaborative enforcement.

Speech to the Chicago Council on Foreign Relations, July 12, 2004

Our enemies are fully aware that they can use oil as a weapon against America. And if we don't take this threat as seriously as the bombs they build or the guns they buy, we will be fighting the war on terror with one hand tied behind our back.

Speech at the Governor's Ethanol Coalition, February 28, 2006

We have utterly failed to deal with what may be one of the most significant potential terror threats to this country, and that is how we protect our chemical plants across the nation.

These plants are stationary weapons of mass destruction spread all across the country. Their security is light, their facilities are easily entered, and their contents are deadly. Unfortunately, the chemical lobby is one of the most powerful ones in Washington. They have dragged their feet, in terms of wanting to move this issue forward. I understand that there is no company out there that wants to be regulated, companies are generally allergic to any intrusion in their business decisions, but this is something of such great importance that we can't afford to rely solely on voluntary measures.

"Improving Chemical Plant Security" podcast, March 29, 2006

ON WASHINGTON, D.C.

What Washington needs is adult supervision.

Fundraising letter, October 2006

When you are in Washington, what struck me was how many really smart, capable people are around you all the time, offering you great ideas on every problem under the sun.

New Yorker, October 30, 2006

When the people running Washington are accountable only to the special interests that fund their campaigns, of course they'll spend your tax dollars with reckless abandon; of course they'll load up bills with pet projects and drive us into deficit with the hope that no one will notice.

Speech to the Chicago Council on Foreign Relations, November 22, 2005

One of the wonderful things about coming to Washington is realizing that everything you do is perceived as calculation. So I can't really spend a lot of time worrying about how my words are interpreted. All I can do is make those words as true as possible.

Morning Edition, July 14, 2006

I am not part of the Washington social set.

National Journal, March 18, 2006

ON WRITING BOOKS

Dreams from My Father was harder to write [than *The Audacity of Hope*.] At that point, I wasn't even sure that I could write a book. And writing the first book really was a process of self-discovery, since it touched on my family and my childhood in a much more intimate way. On the other hand, writing *Audacity* paralleled the work that I do every day: trying to give shape to all the issues that we face as a country, and providing my own personal stamp on them.

Amazon 20-Second Interview, October 2006

The first book was much more introspective. I was digging into sort of my past. It was more a book of self-discovery written by a young man. This book [*The Audacity of Hope*] was more a rumination on the country and where we need to go.

Knight Ridder/Tribune, October 20, 2006

I am somebody who usually writes out the rough draft in longhand. Then I type it into the computer, and that is where I do my editing. I find that if I write it on the computer, I go too quick. So I like getting that first draft out and then typing it in; you are less self-conscious about it.

Chicago Tribune, October 26, 2006

I guess you'd have to say I wasn't a politician when I wrote *Dreams of my Father*. I wanted to show how and why some kids, maybe especially young black men, flirt with danger and self-destruction.

The New Yorker, May 31, 2004

When I sat down to write [*The Audacity of Hope*], my intention was not to write a political manifesto, a 10-point plan for where the country needs to go. The very specific objective of this book was to say there are a set of common values and common ideals that we hold as Americans that need to be excavated, that we need to affirm, that Republicans, Democrats, independents can all buy into.

Charlie Rose Show, October 19, 2006

Even though I hadn't written a book before, I had a sense of what it felt like to write something that rang true. When you start writing you are able to discern where you're being false, where you're using clichés, where you're manufacturing emotion that's not really there, or where you're shying away from something that isn't necessarily flattering.

Men's Vogue, Fall 2006

The Audacity of Hope is not a campaign book. It's me trying to describe the moment I see us being in. Like in my chapter on foreign policy—yeah, I talk about Iraq, but I'm not laying out the ten steps we need to get out of Iraq. I spend more time talking about how, historically, we got to this place.

New York Magazine, October 2, 2006

When I write, I try to be as honest as I could. That's harder when you're in political life, because I think there's a strong impulse to try to control your image as much as possible. I found that the best way for me to approach quote, unquote, "image making" is to be myself and let there everybody know what I'm thinking. And that way, I don't end up tripping myself up saying one thing and doing another.

All Things Considered, October 19, 2006

I would feel very uncomfortable putting my name to something that was written by somebody else or co-written or dictated. If my name is on it, it belongs to me.

Chicago Tribune, March 31, 2006

Acknowledgments

AS USUAL, THANKS first go to Superagent Extraordinaire Scott Mendel.

Thanks also to editor Anita Diggs at Thunder's Mouth Press, who acquired the book.

Kudos to the great electronic databases at Howe Library in Hanover, New Hampshire, and Baker Library at Dartmouth College, which help make papercuts and dusty stacks relics of a past era.

And my eternal thanks to the Salt Hill Pub in Lebanon, New Hampshire, for the burgers, distractions, and endless amusements that always make it easier for me to meet an in-your-face deadline.

About the Author

LISA ROGAK is the author of more than forty books and hundreds of newspaper and magazine articles. She has written biographies on Dr. Robert Atkins, Dan Brown, and Shel Silverstein. She lives in New Hampshire where she is working on a biography on Stephen King.